# From Volcanoes to Islands

## by Rosa Visquel

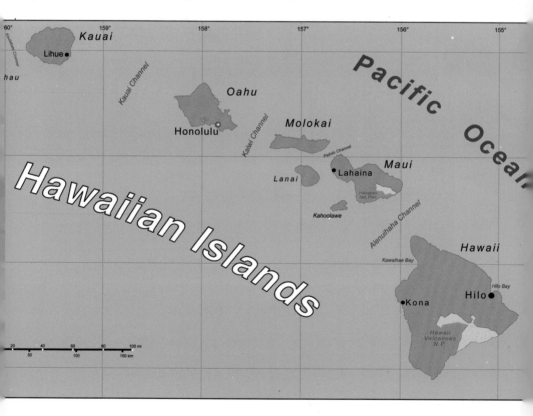

PEARSON

Scott
Foresman

Editorial Offices: Glenview, Illinois • Parsippany, New Jersey • New York, New York
Sales Offices: Needham, Massachusetts • Duluth, Georgia • Glenview, Illinois
Coppell, Texas • Sacramento, California • Mesa, Arizona

A volcanic eruption can be deadly.

It is not safe to be nearby when a volcano erupts. An erupting volcano can kill people and damage property. Volcanoes can do harm, but they can do good things, too. Without volcanoes, we would not have the beautiful state of Hawaii. The Hawaiian Islands began as volcanic eruptions.

---

**erupts:** explodes or violently sends out steam and lava

**islands:** lands surrounded by water

You may have seen pictures of volcanoes erupting on land. Did you know that volcanoes also erupt beneath the deep waters of the sea?

When volcanoes erupt on land, they change the landscape. Underwater volcanoes cause changes, too.

Explosions inside a volcano push lava and rocks out the top of the volcano. When the lava touches ocean water, the lava cools and gets hard.

---

**landscape:** way the land looks

An underwater volcanic eruption

lava

The lava sticks to the sides of the volcano. This makes the volcano's cone grow wider and taller. Every time the volcano erupts, a new layer of lava is added. The volcano grows and grows.

Finally, lava piles up so high that the volcano's tip is above the water. That little tip is the beginning of an island.

As long as the volcano keeps erupting, the island keeps growing.

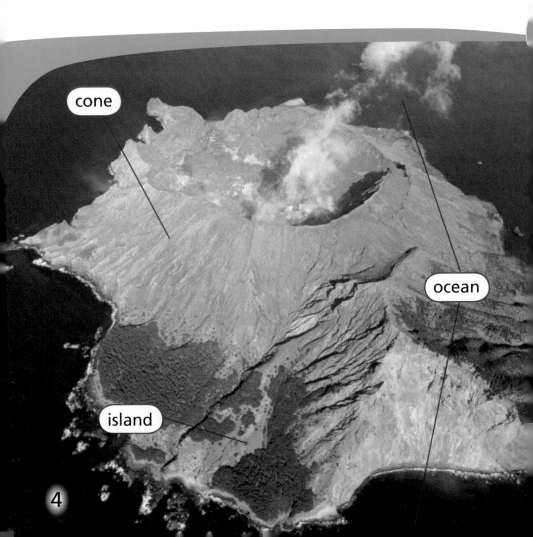

cone

ocean

island

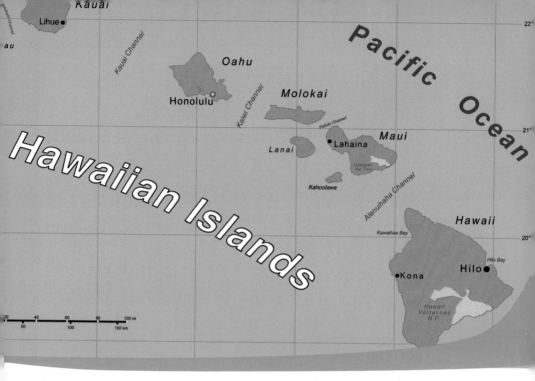

The state of Hawaii is a chain of several islands.

Hawaii began as a group of volcanoes. At first, Hawaii must have looked like piles of rocks sticking up out of the sea. There were no plants or animals.

Finally, most of the volcanoes stopped erupting. Wind and rain beat against the rocky islands. The wind and rain wore down the rock. After a very long time, the surface of the rock turned into sand and soil.

As soon as the islands had soil, they began to change. Birds stopped to rest on the islands. Some of the birds carried seeds. Other seeds floated across the ocean. The seeds began to grow in the new soil.

When plants began growing, birds and other animals were able to find food and shelter on the islands. More and more birds arrived. This time they stayed. Insects and animals also came to the islands.

birds

plant

beach

Finally people arrived, too. The first people sailed from nearby islands. Later, European sailors also discovered the island paradise. Asian people came.

Hawaii's good soil and mild climate make it a perfect place to raise crops. Its beautiful beaches make it a great place to have fun, too.

Like the birds and animals that had arrived earlier, the people decided to stay.

---

**paradise:** place that makes people very happy

Today Hawaii is a busy place. It is filled with people, animals, plants, and beautiful sandy beaches. It is hard to believe that the beautiful islands were once just piles of volcanic rock.

But Hawaiians and visitors know it's true. They say, "*mahalo*," or "thank you," for volcanoes.